MW00339209

JUDAICA

Jewish Coloring Book

for Growns Ups

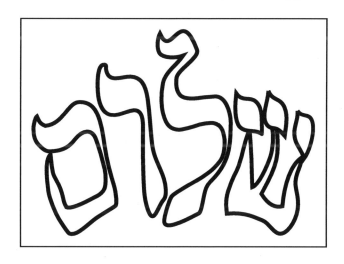

Color for stress relaxation, Jewish meditation,
spiritual renewal, Shabbat peace, and healing.

Aliyah Schick

Sacred Imprints

Other Books by Aliyah Schick

- Jewish Coloring Book: Chai
- Jewish Coloring Book: Alefbet
- Jewish Coloring Book: Star of David

- Meditative Coloring Book 1: Angels
- Meditative Coloring Book 2: Crosses
- Meditative Coloring Book 3: Ancient Symbols
- Meditative Coloring Book 4: Hearts
- Meditative Coloring Book 5: Labyrinths
- Meditative Coloring Book 6: OM

- The Labyrinth Guided Journal: A Year in the Labyrinth

- Mary Magdalene's Words: Two Women's Spiritual Journey, Both Truth and Fiction, Both Ancient and Now.
- The Mary Magdalene Book: Mary Magdalene Speaks, Her Story and Her Message

copyright © 2012 Aliyah Schick, all rights reserved.

Please do not reproduce these images or text.

Thank you for supporting the continuing and future work of creative individuals by honoring copyright laws.

When you buy another book or cd or piece of art, you support and enable its maker to create your next new favorite. Yay!

ISBN: 978-0-9882731-0-8

www.JewishColoring.com

Table of Contents

Dedicated to
peaceful moments,
open hearts,
and
self-discovery.

The Judaica Jewish Coloring Book

The *Judaica Jewish Coloring Book for Grown Ups* is much more than a simple coloring book. It is designed to provide you with an easy, creative path for stress reduction, Jewish meditation, spiritual renewal, Shabbat peace, and healing. Color these beautiful drawings and experience your own deep connection to Jewish heritage, community, and *kavannah*.

The *Judaica Jewish Coloring Book for Grown Ups* celebrates the many familiar symbols and expressions of Judaism: menorah, dreidel, mezuzah, Torah scrolls, ark, Shabbat candles, tree of life, star of David, alefbet, chai, shofar, ten commandments tablets, kiddush cup, shalom, Temple wall, Havdalah candle, Shabbat Shalom, mazel tov, L'shana tova, Ani l'dodi.

These 36 original artist's drawings welcome you to spend quiet, peaceful, meditative time immersed in your Jewish heritage. Perhaps you will discover a new perspective on how Judaism enriches your life.

Judaica

Judaism is a unique mixture of religion and culture. It is a religion, with temples and synagogues, rabbis, services, observances, holy days and holidays, and three main divisions: Orthodox, Conservative, and Reform. And it is a culture, with foods, symbols, language, learning, volunteering and charitable giving, celebrating, and community.

Most non-religious Jews are at least partially culturally Jewish. A little Yiddish, Friday night dinners with wine and candles, chicken soup, potato pancakes with sour cream and apple sauce, Star of David and Chai symbol jewelry, doing good deeds for others, asking questions, lifelong learning. Jewish values are in our bones.

Whether you identify with Reform, Conservative, or Orthodox Judaism, or none of the above, coloring these drawings can beckon you deeper into who you are. Spend some time grounded into your roots. You never know what riches may blossom forth as a result.

What Is Jewish Meditation?

We don't usually think of meditation as Jewish. Most people associate the practice with eastern cultures and religions. Consequently, many modern American Jews who are searching for spiritual meaning or mysticism look outside of mainstream Judaism, not realizing the richness already available within our own heritage. In fact, there is a long history of meditation within Judaism, from biblical times all the way to the present.

Just about any form of meditation has been used and is mentioned in ancient Jewish manuscripts, including mantra meditation, contemplation, using phrases and readings, using an idea, a question, or a point of focus, emptying the mind, or using breath or sound. We don't need to adapt eastern forms of meditation, or even to go into esoteric Kabbalistic and Chasidic forms of meditation. There is plenty of room within Reform, Conservative, and Reconstructionist Judaism for authentic Jewish meditation.

Coloring as Meditation

We won't find coloring specifically mentioned in ancient Jewish writings, but it certainly can be meditative, and it can provide focus on our Jewish roots. Whether coloring is approached as relaxation or as a more intentional means for deepening spiritual connection and awareness, meditative coloring allows the mind and body to quiet busyness and overwhelm, and allows understanding, wisdom, and intuition to expand. When focused on Jewish subject matter, coloring easily fits within other forms of Jewish meditation.

History of Jewish Meditation

According to the *Talmud* and *Midrash*, over a million Jews used to study and practice meditation during the time the *Torah* was written. Up until the 19th century there was widespread meditation among Jews. Then during the Jewish Enlightenment of the 1800's, when the intellectual became valued and the mystical denied, anything mystical, including meditation, was put down as superstition and occult. Even the study of *Kabbalah* was intellectualized, and its deeper meanings were lost. Meditation disappeared from Jewish literature by the end of the 19th century, and its earlier value was forgotten.

Kavannah

The most common term for meditation in Jewish writings is *kavannah*. From the Hebrew root *kavan*, to aim, *kavannah* means directing your consciousness. Usually translated as concentration, feeling, or devotion, *kavannah* in prayer or worship means allowing the words to bring you to the state of consciousness described in the prayer. In other words, direct your consciousness into a meditative state.

The Amidah

The most commonly used Jewish meditation has always been the daily reciting of the *Amidah*. Most modern Jews don't realize that the *Amidah*, especially the first part, was actually designed as meditation. Repeated three times each day, it is a long mantra, lifting us to a higher level of consciousness. Written 2500 years ago by the Great Assembly during the early years of the Second Temple, the *Amidah* was intended to be a standard meditation for every Jew forever. Its carefully composed words create a resonance that brings the person who recites it close to the divine.

"Ribbono shel Olam"

Another commonly used Jewish mantra is "*Ribbono shel Olam.*" This mantra draws our attention to the divine hidden within whatever we are focusing on. The object of attention is then a channel through which we seek and experience the divine. This phrase goes back to biblical times, and was brought to the forefront as a meditation mantra in the early 19th century by Chasidic leader Rabbi Nachman of Bratslav.

The Shema

The *Shema*, Israel's declaration of faith, is to be said twice every day, written in the parchment of the *tefillon* and *mezuzah*, and the last words said before dying. It might seem that the *Shema* would be perfect for a repeating mantra meditation, but the *Talmud* says the *Shema* is not to be used as a repeated mantra. It is meant to be said only once each time. The *shema* could, however, be used in a more fixed, contemplative meditation. Simply focus your entire meditation on the first word, *shema*, and its meaning, "listen" or "hear." Alternatively, contemplate each word, one by one, spending 2 or 3 minutes on each word.

More Information about Jewish Meditation

Within the various historical and present day forms of Jewish meditation there are many possibilities for the modern Jew, whether observant or secular, to find comfortable, effective, and authentically Jewish techniques. For more complete information and specific meditation instructions an excellent resource is the book *Jewish Meditation, A Practical Guide*, by Rabbi Aryeh Kaplan, first published by Schocken Books in 1985.

Making It Yours

Any of these historical forms of Jewish meditation can be combined with coloring to create a meditative practice. You might choose a meaningful mantra word or phrase to repeat silently or softly whisper as you color. Or, begin by reading the weekly Torah portion, then contemplate its message as you color. Or, consider the personal meaning of the drawing's subject matter for you. Put on some beautiful Jewish music, cover your head if that feels right, light candles, wrap yourself in a tallit or shawl, experiment and find what works well for you.

Meditation is very personal, and yet it also connects you with all those millions of Jews, past and present, who have used various forms of meditation to open to and immerse themselves in their faith and culture. Make it yours, and at the same time allow it to deepen your sense of Jewish heritage and belonging.

Suggestions for How to Use This Book

Use this *Jewish Coloring Book* for meditation, spiritual connection, prayer, relaxation, healing, centering, and for coming into your deep, true self. You may simply wish to experience the images in quiet contemplation. Or, you may focus on a Torah portion, a prayer, a phrase, a word, or an affirmation as you work with colors. You may ask for understanding regarding an issue you are dealing with. You may ask for a clearer sense of some aspect of yourself and how it serves you. You may wish to experience a deeper sense of your Jewish heritage and faith. You may wish to cover your head or wrap yourself in a tallit or shawl.

Open your heart and your mind as you use this *Jewish Coloring Book*. Pay attention to impressions and ideas, feelings, intuition, and messages. They may very well be exactly what you need to hear.

Tools

Choose your favorite coloring tools, or you might like to gather a variety of pens, crayons, colored pencils, chalk, oil pastels, markers, glitter pens, paints, etc. You may want to place a blank sheet of paper behind the page so ink or paint does not go through.

Music

Consider playing background music as you color. Try soft instrumental, a heartfelt Jewish singer, or even Klezmer for a more lively experience.

Nature

Sometimes a favorite spot outdoors provides just the right environment for meditation, coloring, and creative expression. Beach, woods, backyard, porch, treehouse, mountain top, stream, pond, park, etc.

Silence

You may prefer quiet, so that all your attention focuses on what you are doing. Emptiness can give rise to profound experience.

Meditation

You may like to meditate first, and then begin working with the colors. Try any of the many ways of meditation, or simply be with your breath for a few minutes, following it in and out. Or, you may wish to try the following meditation. Read it silently or out loud, slowly, pausing to draw in each breath.

A *Ruach* (Breathing) Meditation

• Take in a breath... and on the exhale release the day's happenings, settling into this peaceful time of creative, spiritual connection.

• Take in a breath... and on the exhale let go of worries and troubles and burdens. You can pick them up again later if you need to.

• Take in a breath... and on the exhale come into the center of your Self. From there drop a line down through your body, through the chair and the floor and into the earth. Through soil and sand and stone, through coal and underground stream, and minerals and precious metals. Down through all the colors and textures and densities of the earth, down into the hot magma at this planet's core. Down to the very center of earth and center of the essence of physical being. Tie your line there. Anchor yourself there.

• Take in a breath... and on the exhale extend your line up from your center, through your body and out the crown of your head, up through the ceiling, the roof, and into the sky. Past clouds and wind and thinning gases, out through the atmosphere and into space. Past the sun and galaxy and stars and universe, out to the depths of the source of all that is. Feel your connection there. You are part of the great cosmos. You are one with all being.

• Take in a breath... and on the exhale return to the drawing before you and ask that you be open to receiving guidance and understanding as you spend time with it. Know that there are no mistakes, only new choices and combinations and patterns that suggest new perception at an other-than-conscious level. Or that remind us of something that can now be released. Or that create an opening to new possibilities.

• Take in a breath... and on the exhale release "shoulds" and rules and expectations. Let go and open to new possibilities.

• Now, begin by picking up whatever color catches your attention.

About the Artist

Aliyah Schick has been an artist all of her life. After Peace Corps in the Andes Mountains of South America, she studied art full time for four years, then created and sold pottery and ceramic art pieces for many years. Later Aliyah worked in fiber and fabric, making soft sculptural wall pieces and art quilts, then fabric dolls designed to carry healing energy. Now she draws and paints, and she writes poems and prose.

At the heart of all this, Aliyah's passion is healing. She is a skilled and dynamic deep energetic healer and Transformation Coach. Her work in the multidimensional layers and patterns of the auric field is powerful and effective. Her drawings, paintings, poetry, writings, and books all arise as expressions of Aliyah's healing abilities. Spending time with these drawings serves to bring us back to who we are, where we come from, and why we are here.

Aliyah lives and works in the beautiful Blue Ridge Mountains of North Carolina, where the energy of the earth is easily accessible, ancient, motherly, and obvious. A place where people speak with familiarity and reverence of the land and spirit, and where the sacred comes to sit with us on the porch to share the afternoon sun.

www.AliyahSchick.com

The Drawings

Opposite each drawing is a blank page for your

Notes & Impressions

Use these pages to catch and keep hold of thoughts, wishes, intentions, affirmations, prayers, poems, memories, notes, drawings, or whatever comes to you as you explore coloring with this book. Make it yours.

Shalom   © 2012 Aliyah Schick   13

Candle Light

© 2012 Aliyah Schick   15

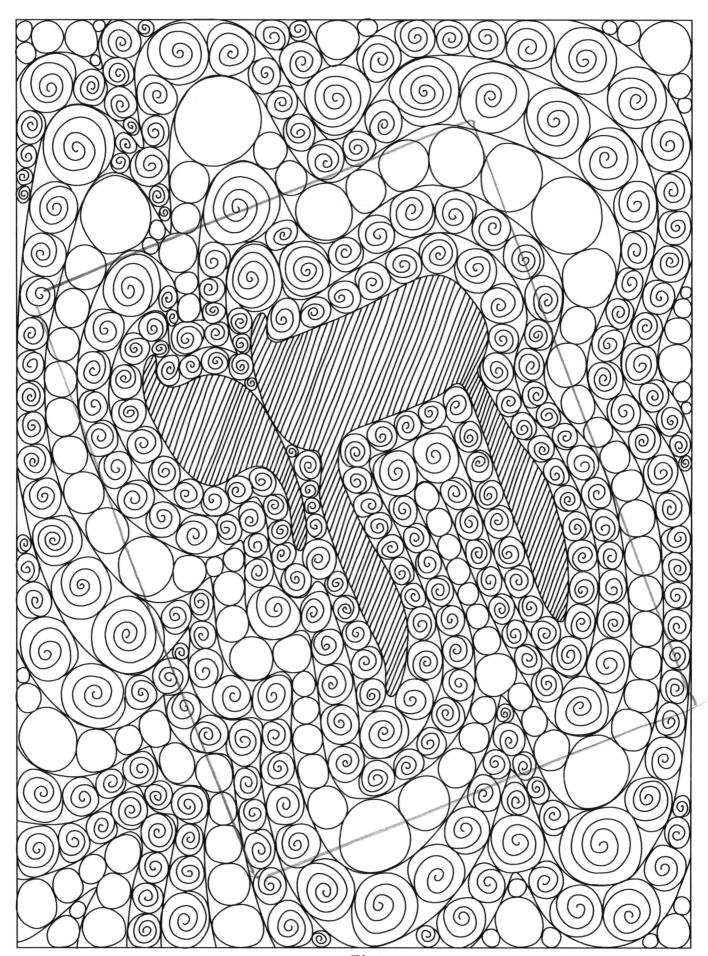

Chai

© 2012 Aliyah Schick   17

Notes & Impressions

Ark and Torah

© 2012 Aliyah Schick

Seven-Candle Menorah   © 2012 Aliyah Schick   21

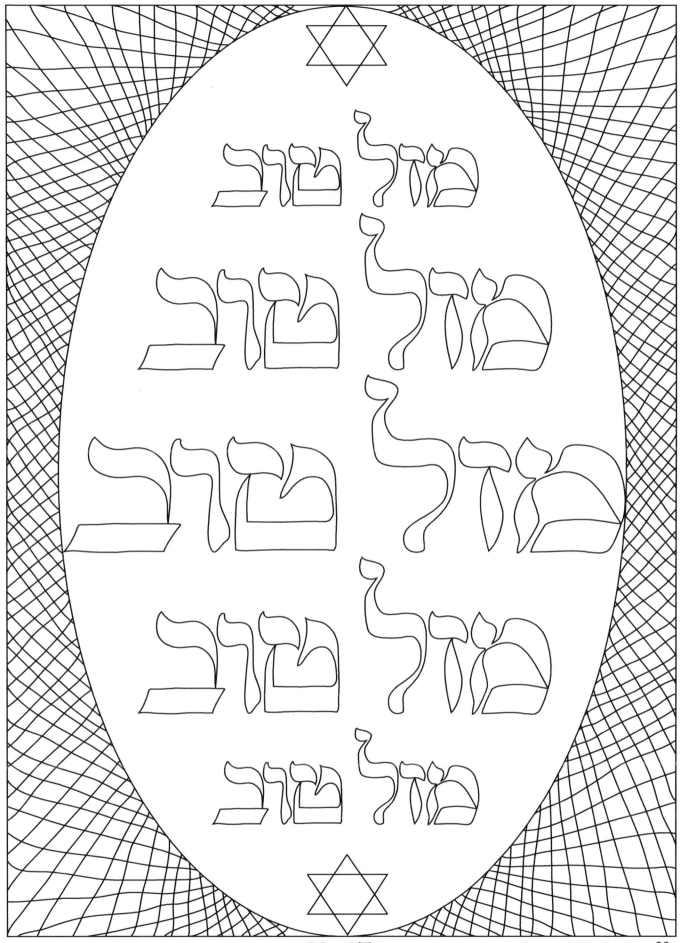

Mazel Tov

© 2012 Aliyah Schick 23

Star of David

© 2012 Aliyah Schick 25

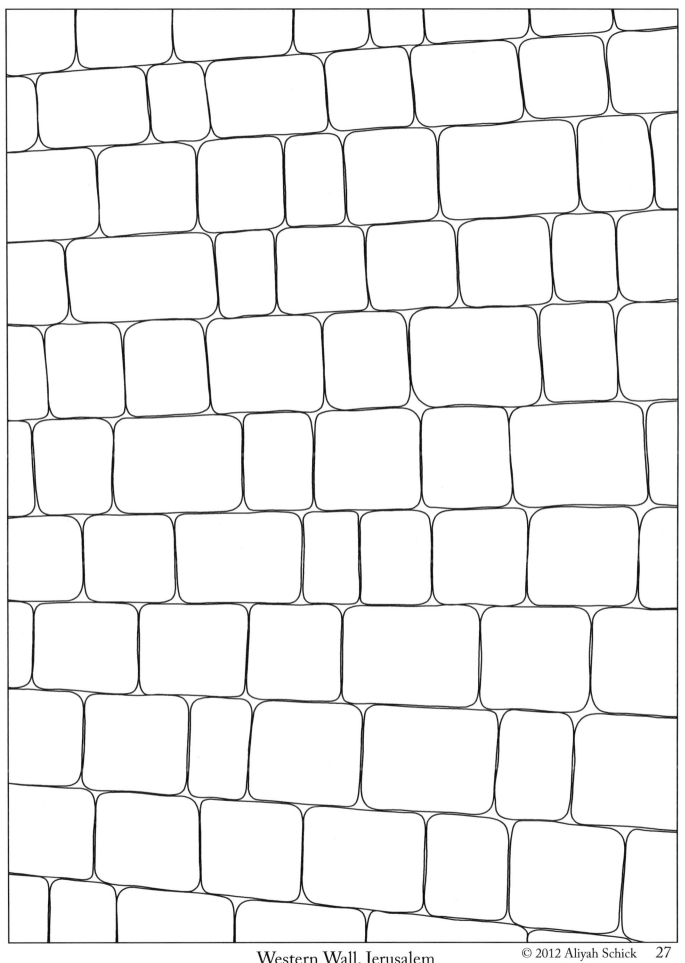

Western Wall, Jerusalem

© 2012 Aliyah Schick 27

Tree of Life   © 2012 Aliyah Schick   29

Shabbat Candles

© 2012 Aliyah Schick 31

Star of David

© 2012 Aliyah Schick 33

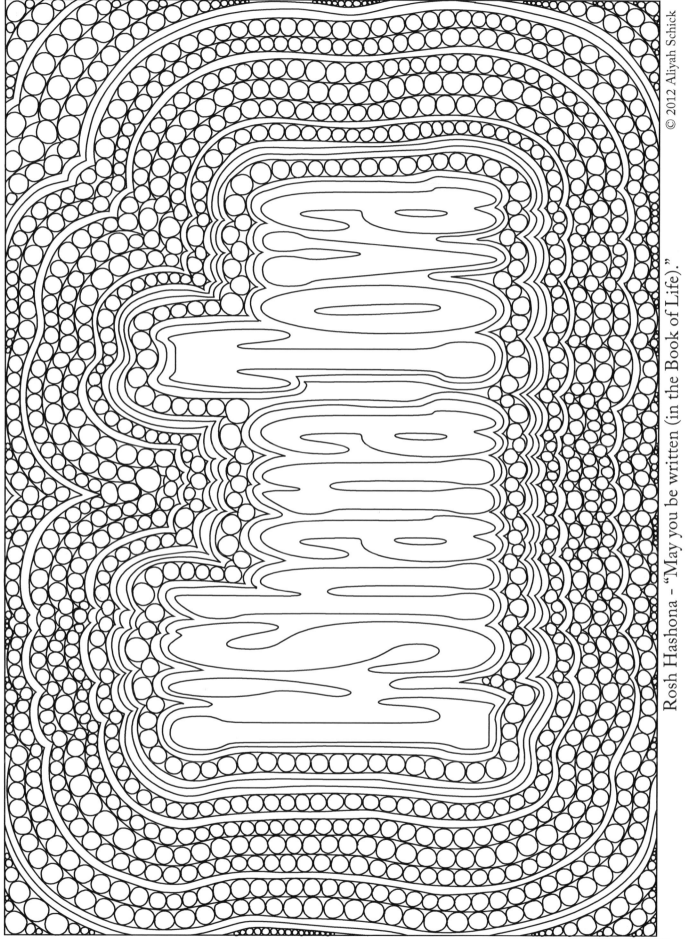

Rosh Hashona – "May you be written (in the Book of Life)."

© 2012 Aliyah Schick

35

Kiddush Cup   © 2012 Aliyah Schick   37

Havdalah Candle

© 2012 Aliyah Schick   39

Ten Commandments Tablets

© 2012 Aliyah Schick

Chanukah Menorah, 9 Candles   © 2012 Aliyah Schick   43

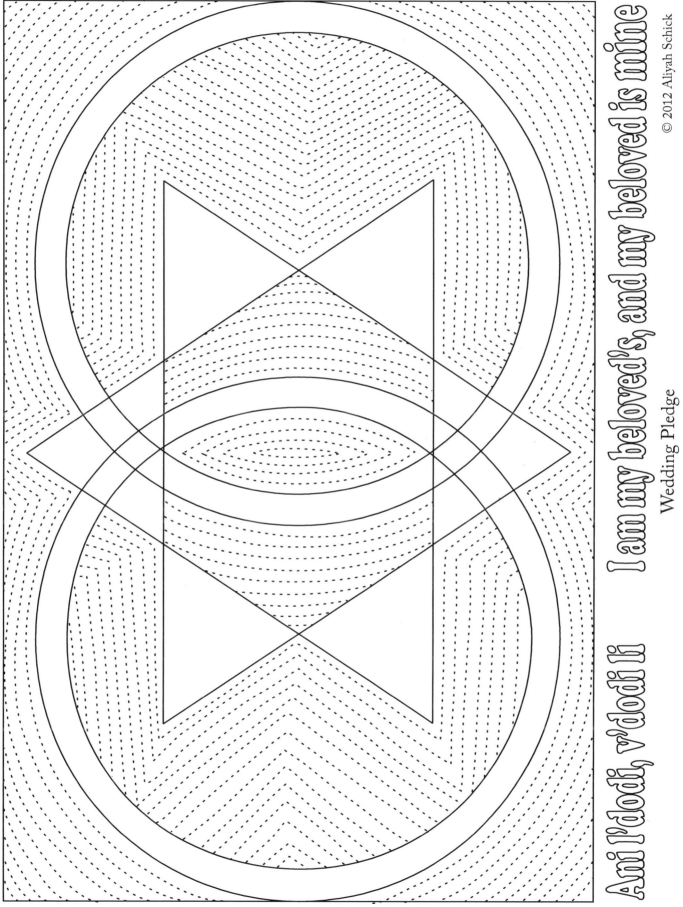

Ani l'dodi, v'dodi li　　I am my beloved's, and my beloved is mine

Wedding Pledge

© 2012 Aliyah Schick

45

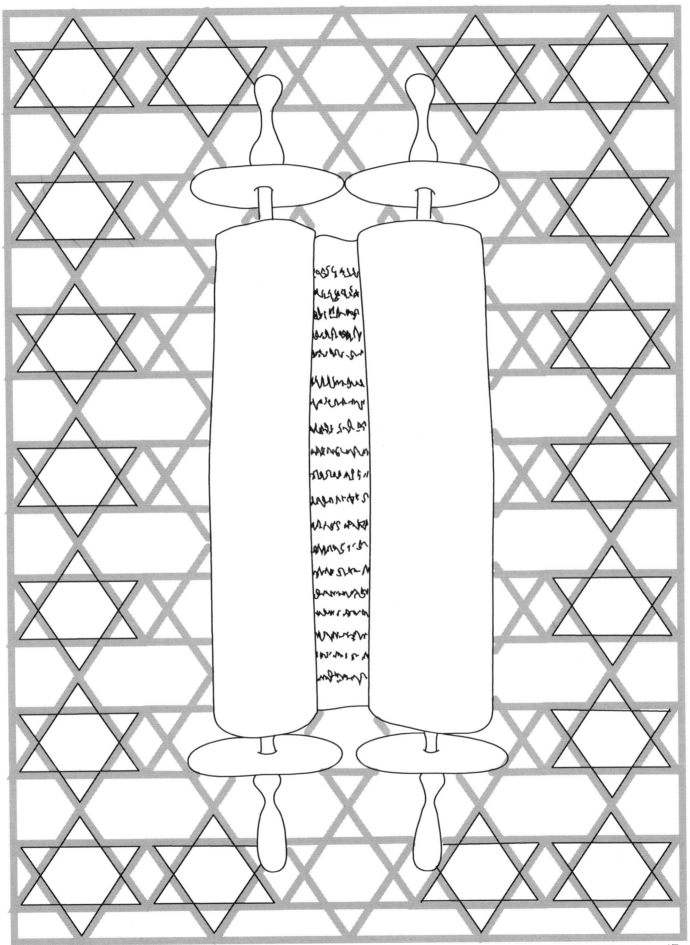

Torah Scroll

© 2012 Aliyah Schick 47

Seven-Candle Menorah   © 2012 Aliyah Schick   51

Chanuka Dreidel   © 2012 Aliyah Schick   53

Candle Light

© 2012 Aliyah Schick   55

Ten Commandments © 2012 Aliyah Schick

Shabbat Shalom　　　© 2012 Aliyah Schick　59

Torah Scroll

© 2012 Aliyah Schick 61

Havdala Candle

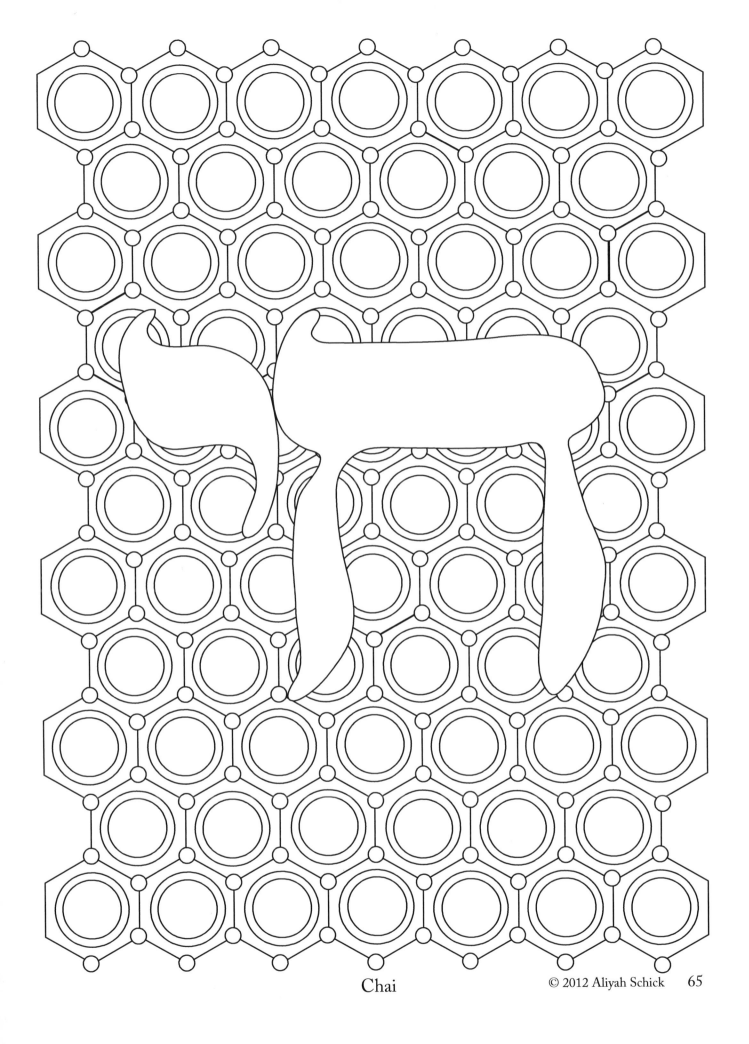

Chai

© 2012 Aliyah Schick

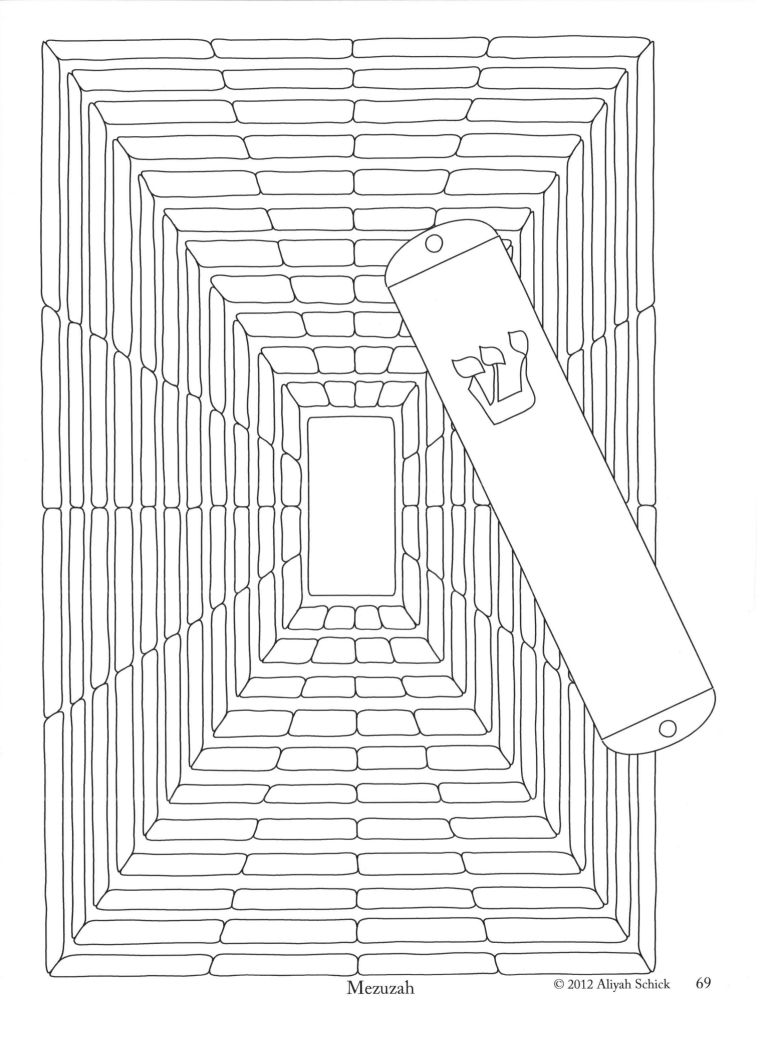

Mezuzah

© 2012 Aliyah Schick

69

Rosh Hashona

© 2012 Aliyah Schick   73

Star of David

© 2012 Aliyah Schick

<u>Notes & Impressions</u>

Tree of Life

© 2012 Aliyah Schick   77

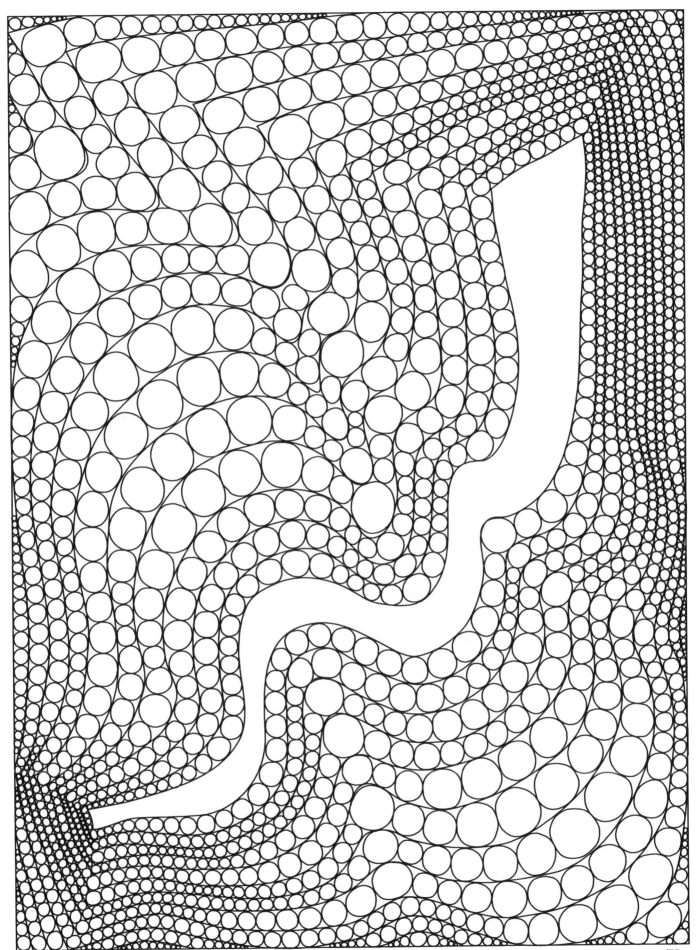

Shofar

© 2012 Aliyah Schick 79

Star of David

© 2012 Aliyah Schick

Shalom

© 2012 Aliyah Schick

83

The Jewish Coloring Books for Grown Ups

Color for stress relaxation, Jewish meditation, Shabbat peace, and healing.

JUDAICA Coloring Book

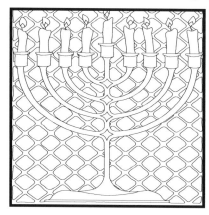

Menorah, dredel, Ten Commandment tablets, challah, Torah scrolls, Magen David, Havdalah braid, mezuzah, and more. Color these beautiful, original artist's drawings based on familiar Jewish objects and symbols. Relax, unwind, de-stress, and allow healing as you ground yourself into your Jewish heritage. L'chaim!

ALEFBET Coloring Book

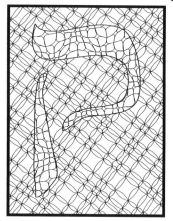

Alef, bet, gimel, dalet, hey, vav, zayin, chet, tet, yod, kaf, lamed, mem, nun, samech, ayin, peh, tsade, qof, resh, shin, and tav; 22 letters in the Hebrew alefbet. Coloring these 36 beautiful, original artist's drawings based on the Hebrew letter forms is relaxing, reduces stress, and lightens your load as it connects you with your Jewish roots. If these letters are the building blocks of the universe, then spending peaceful time coloring them can be beneficial in deeply healing ways, too.

CHAI Coloring Book

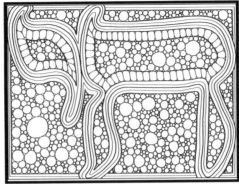

The Jewish *Chai* symbol represents the Hebrew word *chai*, meaning life. It is worn, displayed, or given as a gift as a symbol and reminder of the Jewish love for life, to celebrate being Jewish, and to bring abundant good luck. Spend relaxed, meditative time immersed in the many joys of the *Chai* as you color these 36 beautiful drawings.

STAR OF DAVID Coloring Book

The six-pointed Star of David is our most familiar Jewish symbol. Used as decoration and adornment on both religious and secular items, the Star of David represents Jewish pride in shared heritage, community, and family, and a declaration of hope and commitment. Spend time coloring these 36 original artist's drawings based on the Star of David and allow yourself to ground into your Jewish roots and celebrate your love of being Jewish.

The Meditative Coloring Books Series:
Angels, Crosses, Ancient Symbols, Hearts, Labyrinths, OM

<u>Meditative Coloring Book 1 -- Angels</u>

These angelic images are drawn with a pen in each hand, as artist Aliyah Schick allows the lines to go where they will, mirroring each other. Every movement is guided by spirit; every drawing is different; and each one is a wonderful surprise filled with angelic presence. Immerse yourself in the angelic realm as you color these drawings. Invite the angels to come into your world, to love and support you in all you do.

<u>Meditative Coloring Book 2 -- Crosses</u>

The cross is one of the most ancient and enduring sacred symbols, found in nearly every culture from cave dwellers throughout human existence. It symbolizes the celestial, spiritual divine coming into being in this material world. It represents the sacred taking form, and the integration of soul into physical life. These 36 original artist's drawings feature ancient and contemporary images of the cross in reflections of the deep spiritual significance of its form. Let the spirit and meaning of the cross fill you as you color these images.

Meditative Coloring Book 3 -- Ancient Symbols

Ancient and indigenous sacred images speak deeply to us, to our bellies and our bones, to our cellular memory and our wisdom, to our souls' yearnings. Native peoples throughout time and place see the sacred in all of life. For them, holiness is life and life is holiness. Life is the manifestation of the holy in all things. These original artist's drawings feature timeless designs used by every culture on earth to remind us of the sacred. Dip into deeply meaningful realms as you color these drawings.

Meditative Coloring Book 4 -- Hearts

The heart is one of our favorite symbols, evoking feelings of love, caring, loyalty, and devotion. As you spend time with these heart drawings, open your heart to live with more compassion for others and for yourself. Open your life to deeper connection with the earth and all of life. Open yourself to recognize the sacred in all things, including in yourself.

Meditative Coloring Book 5 -- Labyrinths

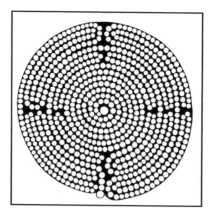

Color your steps into the labyrinth as you contemplate, meditate, or pray. Go deep into your inner wisdom and guidance where questions' answers reveal themselves and choices come clear. Or, simply relax and be with your breathing. Now you can bring your labyrinth with you to wherever you need to be. This collection of 36 original artist's drawings invites you into the labyrinth any time you wish.

Meditative Coloring Book 6 -- OM

Spend meditative time with the *OM* as you color these 36 original artist's drawings. Allow the *OM* to infuse and entune your spirit, your mind, your emotions, and every cell of your body with its pure, sacred grace. Fill yourself with its light. Become one with its beauty. Emerge relaxed, centered, calm, and at peace.

Color for relaxation, stress reduction, meditation, spiritual connection, prayer, centering, and healing. Color to calm and come into balance, to find your intuitive wisdom, and to learn to be more of your deep, true self.

Meditative Coloring Book 7 -- Ancient Goddess

For 30,000 years in prehistoric time people all over the world celebrated and worshipped the sacred feminine. The Great Mother Goddess was the creator of all life and the life force within all life. Worship was every day here and now, holistic, visceral and sensual, all about earth, body, and nature.

Now we are seeing a revival of the sacred feminine through valuing nature, simplicity, mindfulness, meaningfulness, and clarity, along with a growing desire to honor intuition, right-brain knowing, and deep connection.

Color these 36 original artist's drawings as you open yourself to the sacred feminine in you. Nurture this long-abandoned side of conscious living, and bring yourself to a more sustainable balance.

The Labyrinth Guided Journal, a Year in the Labyrinth

The twists and turns of the labyrinth remove you from ordinary life, and draw you deeper into willingness, into yourself, and into sacred wisdom. Use *The Labyrinth Guided Journal* on your own journey through the next year. Each week the journal offers a new thought or experience or challenge drawn from the labyrinth, and a question or suggestion for you to consider and write about throughout the week.

Sacred Imprints